12 THINGS TO KNOW ABOUT
TERRORISM

by Matthew McCabe

12 STORY LIBRARY

www.12StoryLibrary.com

12-Story Library is an imprint of Peterson Publishing Company and Press Room Editions.

Produced for 12-Story Library by Red Line Editorial

Photo Credits: Mark Lennihan/AP Images, cover, 1; Suzanne Plunkett/AP Images, 4, 28; Rafiq Maqbool/AP Images, 5, 29; Shutterstock Images, 6, 11, 17; Thinkstock, 7, 9, 14, 23, 25; adoc-photos/Corbis, 8; Gareth Copley/AP Images, 13; Stocktrek Images/Thinkstock, 15; Tom Horan/AP Images, 16; Jack Affleck/AP Images, 18; Rick Bowmer/AP Images, 19; AP Images, 20; Jacquelyn Martin/AP Images, 22; James Steidl/Shutterstock Images, 24; Donna Beeler/Shutterstock Images, 26; Mark III Photonics/Shutterstock Images, 27

ISBN
978-1-63235-033-6 (hardcover)
978-1-63235-093-0 (paperback)
978-1-62143-074-2 (hosted ebook)

Library of Congress Control Number: 2014946811

Printed in the United States of America
Mankato, MN
October, 2014

Go beyond the book. Get free, up-to-date content on this topic at 12StoryLibrary.com.

TABLE OF CONTENTS

DEFINING TERRORISM IS DIFFICULT

Terrorism is hard to define. It usually centers on a violent act or the threat of violence. Terrorism is about more than just violence, though. Terrorists want to frighten people to achieve a political goal.

Not all violent acts that hurt people can be called terrorism. The attacks of September 11, 2001, are considered terrorism. But the school shooting at Sandy Hook Elementary on December 14, 2012, is not. The terrorists on 9/11 wanted the United States to change its policies in the Middle East. The individual attacker at Sandy Hook did not seek any policy changes. All

People flee from the terrorist attacks on September 11, 2001.

11th

of September, 2001. The date of the worst terrorist attack on US soil.

- Terrorism is difficult to define.
- Terrorists use fear to achieve a political goal.
- Terrorist acts can lead to change if citizens put pressure on their leaders.

TWO SIDES TO THE STORY

What one person calls terrorism might not be called the same by another person. Some attackers think their violent actions are justified. Imagine two insurgents plant a road-side bomb in Afghanistan. The bomb injures or kills US troops. Americans might call it a "terrorist act." But the insurgents would say they were defending their home from invaders.

terrorist acts have something in common: fear. Attackers try to use fear to force a change in how people behave. Leaders might not change policies because of terror attacks. But if large groups of citizens become fearful, they might ask leaders for change. This makes terrorism popular among groups without power. Terrorists cannot fight back against stronger opponents. But they can cause chaos and create fear by attacking innocent people.

A US soldier and a bomb-sniffing dog search for roadside bombs in Afghanistan in 2009.

RISK OF DEATH IS LOW

Terrorism works by creating fear. The fear of injury or death is powerful. Terrorists want to use that fear to change behavior. But the risk of death from terrorism is low. Most people will never be affected by terrorism.

It is common to be frightened after an attack. But the truth is that other dangers have greater risks. More Americans suffer heart problems than die from terrorism. People are more likely to be harmed by lightning than by terrorism.

The number of terror attacks in the United States is very low. Many attacks that do happen do not target people. People who travel

Lightning injures more people than acts of terrorism do.

16

Number of terror attacks, carried out or plotted, in New York City since 2001.

- The odds of being impacted by terrorism are extremely low.
- Americans are increasingly aware today. This improves safety.
- Governments are getting better at preventing terror attacks.

they travel, they are avoiding places where terrorism is high. This lowers their risk of injury or death.

The US government has made changes to protect people better, too. Police train differently now. Police officers are more aware of public behavior. Law enforcement groups now work together more than in the past.

are making smarter choices. Because Americans can be targets when

Police are now trained to look for unusual behavior in public places.

TERRORISM IS NOT NEW TO THE WORLD

There have been many terrorist attacks in recent years. But terrorism is not new. People have used violence against others for a long time. Using violence to create fear also has a long history. In the past, there was no name for these types of violent acts.

The assassination of Paris mayor Jacques Flesselles is one example of violence in the French Revolution.

The first time violence was described as terrorism was 1795. During the French Revolution, the term "terrorism" began to appear in writing. Many violent acts took place in France at this time. Each time, innocent people were the targets. That violence was used to create fear in the French people.

By bombing buildings, terrorists target many people at once.

219

Years since the word "terrorism" was first used to describe violence against citizens.

- The modern idea of terrorism came from the French Revolution.
- Forcing change was the original goal of terrorism.
- Terror methods have changed over the past two centuries.

The attackers hoped fear would force a change in French politics.

History shows that terrorism is not new. The methods used to create terror are different today. In the past, terrorists killed individuals. Now, many terrorists use bombings that can target many people. But the goal today is the same as the goal in the past. Terrorists use violence to spread fear and create change with that fear.

TERRORISM HAS UNPREDICTABLE EFFECTS

Lots of people have been hurt by terrorism. But this does not mean terrorists get the changes they hoped for.

Major terror attacks are designed to change policies. The attacks of September 11, 2001, were meant to change US policies in the Middle East to reduce US involvement in the region. But America is now more involved in the Middle East than before. US forces have fought two wars in Iraq and Afghanistan since then. This was not the change terrorists wanted to occur. Instead of leaving the Middle East, the US increased its presence there.

Another change happened as a result of the 9/11 attacks. Because the attackers hijacked airplanes

WHY THE MIDDLE EAST?

The United States has been involved in the Middle East since the end of World War I in 1918. It tries to protect what it sees as its interests in the Middle East. Historically, these have been oil and the political structure of Middle Eastern countries. Some people in the Middle East do not want the United States involved in their countries.

to use as weapons, some people became afraid to fly. New safety measures were put in place for airlines. These new safety measures created higher costs for airlines. Airlines charged passengers more money to cover those costs. Now, the cost of flying is much higher.

Terrorists did not attack the United States to make flying more expensive. They did it to change US policies in the Middle East. In this case, the terrorists did not achieve their original goal. But the fear they created did lead to other changes.

130

Estimated number of terrorism-related laws introduced in Congress in the year after the 9/11 attacks.

- Terrorism can lead to changes in policy.
- Sometimes the changes that occur are not intended.
- The attacks of September 11, 2001, led to many changes in the United States.

The 9/11 attacks resulted in higher costs for airplane passengers.

TERRORISM AFFECTS THE WHOLE WORLD

Acts of terror can happen anywhere. Terrorism is common in war zones. But it can also happen in peaceful countries. Terrorism is often viewed as a problem in the Middle East. But no part of the world is safe from terrorism.

Attacks in the United States have made Americans uncomfortable. But the United States is targeted far less than other countries. There were 2,608 terror attacks in the United States between 1971 and 2011. North Africa and the Middle East suffer the most. There have been 23,089 attacks in those regions since 1971.

Terrorist attacks happen for different reasons. The reasons often depend on the region. Attackers can be motivated by politics. Others are motivated by religion. Terrorists use violence to force policy changes in their own countries. Others might use violence to gain attention for a cause.

Other terror attacks are based on revenge. In July 2005, terrorists bombed the transit system in London, England. These Muslim British citizens were unhappy with the British government for going to war in Iraq.

Armenia Azerbaijan
key   Sea   Turkmenistan
Syria
Iraq   Iran   Af
Jordan
Gulf of Aqaba
Kuwait   Persian
Gulf
Saudi Arabia
Red   12
Sea
Eritrea

The Middle East is a region found in southwestern Asia.

MANY REASONS

There can be multiple reasons for a terror attack. One example is the bombing of a Bali night club in 2002. Local terrorists wanted to create a state based in Islamic law. But they chose a popular tourist spot so they could strike foreign visitors, too. This gave the attackers attention across the world. That attack was part of seven bombings in a three-week span.

700

Estimated number of people injured in the July 2005 London bombings.

- Americans are not the only targets of terrorism.
- Sometimes, terrorists target their own countries to create change.
- Terrorists use violence to draw attention to a cause.

Many British Muslims spoke out against the actions of terrorists in London.

6

BOMBINGS ARE A COMMON TOOL

One terrorist tool has proven more common than others. Bombings have become the top choice of terrorists. Bombs were used in 52 percent of attacks in the United States from 1970 to 2011. Poison gas and gun violence have become less common.

Terrorists use bombs to frighten people. Bombs leave a large physical mark. Following a bombing, buildings can be destroyed or damaged. Roads can be blocked by massive holes. A bombing attracts a lot of media attention. Cameras can focus in on the damage. Spectacular images of destruction can help spread the terrorists' message.

Bombs can destroy homes and other buildings.

US soldiers practice defending themselves against a poison gas attack.

There are other reasons bombings are so common. People with guns are limited by the number of bullets they have. One bomb could hurt hundreds of people at one time. Poison gas could have the same impact. But controlling poison gas can be more difficult.

Any of these actions can create fear. A shooting spree in a public place frightens people. Poison gas cannot be seen or heard. That makes a gas attack frightening. But bombings remain the most common.

THINK ABOUT IT

Reread these two pages. What is the main idea? Write it down on a piece of paper. Then, find three pieces of evidence that support the main idea. List them under the main idea on your paper.

23

Number of people affected by anthrax attacks in the United States in fall 2001.

- Terrorists use a number of tools for violence.
- Bombings are the most common terrorist tool.
- Other tools are more lethal, but bombings create fear quickly.

7

TERROR ATTACKS STILL HAPPEN IN THE UNITED STATES

Terrorist acts continue to happen in the United States. So far, none of these attacks have been on the same scale as the ones on 9/11. Terrorists still want to frighten people. But doing so does not always require a bomb's destruction. An attack on a piece of property can have the same impact.

There were 207 attacks in the United States between 2001 and 2011. Most of those attacks did not harm innocent people. Instead, more than half of them targeted properties in the United States. These attacks were meant to disrupt life and create confusion.

The Pentagon, the headquarters of the US Department of Defense, was attacked on September 11, 2001.

Some terrorists target laboratories that use animals to test products.

The type of target is different based on the terrorist. Some attacks are against government facilities. Other attacks are against transportation systems such as buses and trains. In 1980, a bomb was set off in Penn Station in New York. The goal was to disrupt the rail system in the region. In 1977, there was an explosion on the Route 1 bridge connecting Homestead and Key West, Florida.

207
Terror attacks in the United States between 2001 and 2011.

- Domestic terrorism rarely targets civilians.
- Transportation and government facilities are popular targets.
- The goal of domestic terrorism is to disrupt daily life.

NO INJURIES NECESSARY

Terrorism does not need to cause harm to innocent people. Attacks on airlines and airports disrupt travel. Businesses can be targeted for various reasons. Extreme animal rights groups may attack businesses that test new products on animals. These types of terrorism are still used in the United States. But the goal is not physical harm. The goal is confusion and hurting the economy.

8

TERRORISTS ARE A DIVERSE GROUP OF PEOPLE

Since September 11, 2001, most people fear al-Qaeda. This group was responsible for the 9/11 attacks. The attacks led people to believe terrorists only belong to groups like al-Qaeda. But not all terror groups share al-Qaeda's beliefs. Terrorist groups come in all types.

Ecoterrorism is a common form of violence. Ecoterrorist groups believe humans do too much harm to the environment. They use terror to protest the government's environmental policies. People are rarely harmed in ecoterrorism attacks. Ecoterrorists do not want to hurt people. They want to stop activities that harm the environment. They use terrorism to stop these activities. One example is the Earth Liberation Front (ELF). The ELF targets businesses that harm the environment.

ELF burned down this building at a ski resort in Vail, Colorado.

OTHER TERRORIST GROUPS

Al-Qaeda gets a lot of attention. But other groups have attacked the United States more often. The ELF has used terrorism 50 times since 2001. An animal rights group, the Animal Liberation Front, has used it 34 times. No one was hurt in these attacks, so these events do not get much attention in the media.

167

Number of deaths in the Oklahoma City bombing.

- Various groups use terrorism.
- Ecoterrorism is common in the United States.
- Not all terrorists share the same views and beliefs.

However, groups are not the only ones who use terrorism. Individuals use it, too. Timothy McVeigh bombed a government building in Oklahoma City on April 19, 1995. He viewed the government as repressive. His solution was to use terrorism for revenge.

FBI agents investigate the Oklahoma City bombing site.

19

9

GOVERNMENTS CAN BE INVOLVED IN TERRORISM

The airplane bombing left its mark on Lockerbie, Scotland.

270

Number of people killed in the Lockerbie bombing.

- Governments play an important role in protecting citizens.
- Past government actions during wartime have been labeled terrorism.
- Some governments sponsor terror attacks, directly or indirectly.

Protection is an important role of any government. Police work to keep streets safe. Firefighters work to prevent fires from destroying homes. The military protects a country's borders and other interests.

However, governments have also been accused of acts of terrorism. Many of these actions took place during a war. Others took place during a time of peace. People develop different views on actions based on when they occur. Some believe violent action during war is acceptable. Others view all violence against civilians as terrorism.

THINK ABOUT IT

Should actions during war count as terrorism? Decide yes or no. Then, defend your decision using evidence from the rest of this book.

Here are two different examples of government actions that might be considered terrorism. An airplane blew up over Lockerbie, Scotland, in 1988. The government of Libya was blamed for the attack. During World War II, US forces firebombed Dresden, Germany. The town was completely destroyed. One act took place during a time of peace. The other act took place during war.

Both attacks hurt innocent people. The victims of both attacks considered them acts of terrorism. But the Libyan government and US government thought their actions were justified. Both attacks created fear. It is possible to consider the Lockerbie bombing and the bombing of Dresden acts of terror.

GOVERNMENTS ALSO WORK TO PREVENT TERRORISM

Governments use many tools to prevent terrorism. Some are used outside the United States to stop terrorists. Other are used inside the country. While some of these tools are visible to the public, others are not.

The War in Afghanistan is a good example of a visible tool. People followed the progress of US troops in the country. US forces prevented terrorism in Afghanistan in many ways. They pushed out terrorists hiding in the country. The forces also helped Afghanistan protect itself. US soldiers trained members of the Afghan army. The US government provided Afghanistan with money to rebuild and prevent terrorism.

The leaders of various US intelligence agencies gather to discuss threats to the country.

Other tools are not as visible to the public as a war. In the United States, the Federal Bureau of Investigation (FBI) and Central Intelligence Agency (CIA) share information. Instead of trying to prevent attacks alone, they work together. The government also created new agencies to fight terror. The Department of Homeland Security protects the nation from threats. The National Counterterrorism Center is a new idea to combat terror. This group provides a central location to share information. It allows multiple groups to work together to prevent attacks.

Not all tools prevent terrorism the same way. Better security at airports prevents terrorism on airlines. The use of drone aircraft provides information. These planes can track terrorists anywhere. Drones are designed to combat many types of terrorism. Despite their differences, all these tools help prevent terrorism.

$2 trillion

Amount the United States spent fighting in Afghanistan and Iraq between 2001 and 2013.

- Communication within the government helps fight terrorism.
- New agencies have been created to focus on terrorism.
- Not all tools for preventing terror are seen and felt.

THINK ABOUT IT

Do you think these different tools make the country safer? Decide yes or no. Then, use information in this book and another source to provide at least three reasons to support your answer.

LAW ENFORCEMENT IS IMPROVING

Terror attacks are designed to make people feel unsafe. If people do not feel safe, they change their behavior. It is the job of law enforcement to ensure everyone feels safe. Their actions can block terrorists from reaching their goals.

Law enforcement must be able to uncover terrorists' plans before they happen. Sharing information between law enforcement officials helps uncover potential attacks. With more information before an attack, action can be taken to prevent it.

Law enforcement and the public work together. People have become more aware in public places. When they see something suspicious, they alert law enforcement. The two sides work together to prevent attacks.

Airport security checks are one way the public helps law enforcement prevent terrorism.

Law enforcement officials share information to help fight terrorism.

It is not possible to prevent all terrorism. But law enforcement in the United States has improved. The total number of attacks is declining. The number of successful attacks is also declining. Better information is being collected and shared. Law enforcement's reaction times are improving because of that information. The result is a safer United States.

44

Percentage of terror plots thwarted by US law enforcement in 2011.

- Law enforcement agencies are becoming better at preventing terrorism.
- Not all terrorist attacks can be prevented.
- The public plays a role in preventing terror through vigilance.

THE INTERNET IS TERRORISM'S NEW FRONTIER

For many years, terrorist attacks have involved physical weapons. Terrorists have used bombs, poison gas, and even airplanes to carry out their attacks. Recently, they have started to use a new tool: the Internet.

Intelligence agencies call the use of the Internet to commit terrorist acts *cyberterrorism*. Cyberterrorists use the Internet to harm or destroy important information and data. This information may include details on the government's counterterrorism efforts. Computer programs that manage and control airplanes, trains, and other means of transportation can be attacked. Cyberterrorists may also target energy industry computer networks. When they attack, cyberterrorists try to destroy or disable computer programs. Sometimes, these programs control machinery or other equipment. An attack could shut down the equipment, which may cause an emergency, such as a fire or explosion. These events could cause injuries and deaths.

Cyberterrorism can disrupt air travel.

Many intelligence experts agree most cyberterrorist attacks do not put the public in physical danger. But the attacks can cause disruptions in daily life. They can also make people feel unsafe. Attacks on an airline's computer network may cause travel delays and cancellations. An attack on a city's 911 computer system would make it difficult for people to get help. These attacks may not physically harm someone. But they do make daily life more difficult.

Cyberterrorists use the Internet to commit terrorist acts.

THE MASK

In February 2014, Internet security company Kaspersky Lab discovered a cyberterrorist threat called the Mask. Kaspersky Lab predicted the Mask would attack the computer programs and data of oil and natural gas companies. Since 2007, the Mask has attacked thousands of computers with Internet connections. These computers have been in dozens of countries.

0

Number of people killed or injured by cyberterrorists through November 2012.

- Cyberterrorists use the Internet to commit terrorist acts.
- Often, these acts target the computer programs and systems of governments or of the energy and transportation industries.
- Most experts agree that cyberterrorism does not put the public in physical danger.

27

FACT SHEET

- No two nations define terrorism the same way. In the United States, the FBI and CIA use different definitions for terrorism. Some of the United States' allies use different definitions than those used in the United States. The United Kingdom does not use the word "violence" in its definition of terrorism. Instead, the term "criminal activity" appears more often. The European Union and United Nations also use different terms and phrases to describe terrorism. This lack of common terms makes it hard for the world to agree on a clear definition.

- Victims describe actions taken by the US government during World War II as acts of terrorism. US forces used firebombs to create chaos in Tokyo, Japan. This tactic was devastating in Japan because of the number of buildings constructed entirely of wood. The most discussed action of World War II was the use of two atomic bombs. The towns of Hiroshima and Nagasaki, Japan, were hit with atomic bombs. The goal was to force Japan to surrender. This

choice is criticized because the towns had little military value. Thousands of innocent Japanese people died in the attacks.

- Prior to September 11, 2001, Timothy McVeigh was responsible for the worst terror attack in US history. When he set off a bomb inside a truck in Oklahoma City, Oklahoma, 167 people died and 600 were injured. Unlike recent attacks against the United States, McVeigh was an American. He was frustrated with government power in the United States. His anger was over the deaths of 76 people during a government siege of a property in Waco, Texas. McVeigh targeted the Alfred P. Murrah Federal Building as revenge for that siege. His action remains the most serious act of domestic terrorism in US history.

GLOSSARY

al-Qaeda
A terror group that has been responsible for many acts of terrorism against the United States.

anthrax
Bacteria that causes a serious infectious disease that often leads to death in humans.

counterterrorism
Government activities designed to prevent terrorism.

facilities
Buildings used for a specific purpose.

firebombed
Used bombs to create intense heat and large fires.

insurgents
People who fight against a government or other authority.

law enforcement
A label for various government groups that make sure laws are followed.

motivated
Have a reason for doing something.

public
Relating to all the people of a state or country.

revenge
Taking action to hurt someone because they hurt you.

terrorist
Someone who uses violence to create fear and chaos.

violence
The use of physical force to harm someone or something.

FOR MORE INFORMATION

Books

Brown, Don. *America Is Under Attack: September 11, 2001: The Day the Towers Fell*. New York: Roaring Brook Press, 2011. Print.

Horn, Geoffrey M. *FBI Agent*. Pleasantville, NY: Gareth Stevens Publishing, 2009. Print.

Sterngass, Jon. *Terrorism*. New York: Marshall Cavendish Benchmark, 2012. Print.

Websites

FBI's Fun and Games Site
www.fbi.gov/fun-games

National Counterterrorism Center's Kids Zone
www.nctc.gov/site/kids/index.html

Terrorism
www.kidshealth.org/kid/feeling/thought/terrorist_attacks.html

INDEX

About the Author

Matthew McCabe is a freelance writer with years of experience. He has written several magazine articles, contributes to business blogs, and creates marketing content for numerous businesses. He lives in Plymouth, Minnesota.

32